Mindset Makeover

How Small Changes Can Unlock Your Potential

Bob Wilson

Dedicated to two very special people:

Harry Wilson and Brooke Nordstrom.

You both hold a very special place in my heart.

Dad, you left this world way too soon.

Your presence and the lessons you taught are with me daily.

Brooke, my daughter, the door is always open.

Walk through when you are ready.

I am waiting with open arms.

Table of Contents

Introduction

You have been misled.

Your mindset has been right in the middle of it. Before I explain how you've been misled, let me first define what mindset is.

Your mindset is a collection of beliefs and assumptions you have about other people and the world around you.

One way to think of it is as a filter through which you view things around you.

Your mindset affects your thoughts, feelings, decisions and actions. Your mindset is powerful.

You have been conditioned to react based on your mindset. Your mindset becomes so familiar that it functions without you even thinking about it.

Your mindset is shaped by family, friends, school, work, society and yourself.

Despite everyone's good intentions, certain mindsets are accepted as true, but really aren't (e.g. multitasking doesn't make you more productive; morc on this later).

Other mindsets work well in certain situations, but we apply them in situations where we shouldn't.

With mindset there is both good news and bad news.

The good news is it helps us be more efficient. We don't have to agonize and reflect over every single decision. Our mindset helps us to act and react more decisively.

The bad news I stated earlier: some assumptions are either incorrect or applied where they shouldn't be. This is what I call a misplaced mindset.

An example of a misplaced mindset is thinking you can achieve happiness by pursuing it directly. Happiness is best found indirectly (more on this later).

Mindset Makeover helps you examine your mindset more closely to discover where your mindset is working against you. In each chapter, I cover opposing mindsets and the shifts that can help you unlock your potential.

By being more aware of your mindset, it is easier to make adjustments that lead to greater success and increased fulfillment.

A Full Schedule *versus* A Full Life

A Full Schedule

Many people work hard to fill every single moment of their life. Then they either complain about how busy they are or brag about it.

This is a crazy way to live your life.

We have been conditioned to believe that busy equates to self-worth: the busier you are, the worthier you are.

That is messed up.

A mindset that includes, "I have to always be busy" is the surest way to overwhelm, stress and burnout.

"Busy" is a bad habit. What will it take for you to want to break it?

Don't wait for burnout before you turn things around. It is time now to stop this never-ending pursuit of busy.

A great first step is to take a break. Even five minutes can make a big difference. Sit still and do nothing. Close your eyes for a moment and relax. It is easy to forget how refreshing a brief stop can be.

A common objection I hear is: If I take a break I will fall farther behind and be more stressed. This usually of symptom of another issue: Saying "yes" to too many things. I cover this in the next chapter.

I challenge you to go a week without telling anyone that you are busy. See if you can do it. It is much tougher than you think.

A Full Life

A full life isn't one that is constantly busy. A full life is a quality life.

Don't make life about filling moments, make it about moments that are full.

Often we get confused that "big things' are what lead to a quality life. Usually it is the small things that add quality to your life.

Become better at spotting the small things in life and you will have a fuller, more meaningful life.

Also, a helpful exercise is to make a list of the things that are most important to you. Then list how much time you spend on each.

If these important things aren't getting as much time as they should, make a list of where you are spending your time.

Create a plan to decrease the time you spend on these less important tasks so you have more time for the important things.

Key Takeaways:

Don't equate being busy with your self-worth.

A mindset that includes "I have to always be busy" is the surest way to overwhelm, stress and burnout.

"Busy" is a bad habit. What will it take for you to want to break it?

Try going one week without telling anyone you are busy.

Stop and think about why you are doing all the things that make your life non-stop busy. Write down the reasons. Create a plan to make the changes you want and need to make.

Actively look for ways to slow down and include breaks throughout your day. Some examples:

- Create some "do nothing" time each week. Just relax and do nothing. You will be surprised how refreshing just 10 or 15 minutes of this time can be.

- Go for a walk without your phone. Take time to notice the beauty of nature around you.
- Schedule a day or a weekend to "unplug" from technology.
- Put your to-do list aside for a few minutes and spend time "being" instead of "doing."
- While stopped at a traffic light or waiting in line somewhere instead of using your phone to check email or Facebook, just relax and take a few deep, relaxing breaths.
- Turn off the TV. It doesn't have be off all the time. Chances are it is on a lot more than it needs to be.
- Take the time to notice when your mind gets more easily distracted. This is a sign that it is time for you to take a break.

Being a People-Pleaser *versus* Having Boundaries

Being a People-Pleaser

Pleasing other people feels good. Pleasing others isn't a bad thing, but when it becomes your primary goal, it works against you.

Chronic people-pleasers have very little time for themselves. Oftentimes they end up resenting the very people they are trying to please.

Instead of being a chronic people-pleaser, start with pleasing yourself. This will make you stronger and better able to help those around you.

I like to compare it to when a flight attendant reminds you to use an oxygen mask on yourself first so you are strong enough to help others.

Having Boundaries

Our society is focused on everything: do everything, be everything and have everything.

The "everything" mindset means you don't have boundaries. This is unhealthy. Ironically, this mindset usually leads to a life full of "busy," but not much else.

Having healthy boundaries means you set limits. You set a clear understanding of what you will and won't put up with. You learn to have a better balance between saying "yes" and "no."

There are times where "yes" is the best choice. But a mindset of saying "yes" to nearly everyone and everything, leads to:

- Overload
- Stress
- Inefficiency
- Burnout

In this case, your boundaries have thinned or disappeared. Boundaries are healthy. Boundaries help you be your best self.

> *"As I look back on my life, it has always been saying 'no' to something that has been the first step in each of my most powerful emotional and spiritual transformations."*
> ~ Barbara De Angelis

<u>Key Takeaways</u>:

Boundaries help you be your best self.

Finding the right balance between "yes" and "no" takes effort and focus. In today's information-overloaded world it is more important than ever to find the right balance. To improve the balance between "yes" and "no" in your life, do the following exercise:

- Draw a line down the middle of a piece of paper. For the next week, write down everything you say "yes" to in the left column.

- Remember to include even the implied "yes." For example, if you tell your child to clean his room and then you do it for him, this is an implied "yes," so write it in the left column.

- After the week is up, in the right-hand column list other possible actions you could have taken with each "yes." So, with the example of the child not cleaning their room, in the right-hand column you might write things like: Ask them again, take away his allowance, ground her, etc.

Now look at your list and see if there are any patterns:

- Is there an option you regularly avoid (e.g. delegation)?
- Is there anyone you always say "yes" to?

Notice the number of things you say "yes" to that have at least two other alternatives. Quite a few, isn't it?

Procrastination *versus* Action

Procrastination

Procrastination is no stranger to any of us. For some it is a casual acquaintance. For others it is a dear friend.

People sometimes think they procrastinate because they are lazy or there is something wrong with them. Neither of these is a primary cause of procrastination.

Procrastination can be driven by many things. Here are five of the main reasons people procrastinate:

1. Fear of criticism
2. Being a perfectionist
3. Having a victim mentality or anger issues
4. Being easily distracted (hint: we all are, that's part of being human)
5. Ego – You finish a task last minute and people praise you.

You finish it early and few, if any, even notice.

One day, roughly twenty years ago, I decided I'd had enough of my dear friend, procrastination.

I read as much as I could find on procrastination. As a result, I discovered three big surprises:

1. The cure for procrastination is simple. No rocket science needed.
2. I was procrastinating a lot, but once I looked closer, it was much worse than I realized. Part of the reason for this is procrastination is sneaky (more on this is later).
3. Once I started conquering procrastination in one area of my life, I procrastinated less in other areas too. With procrastination it's either an upward or downward spiral. That is, let procrastination run

wild in your life, then with any
new activity, you are more
likely to procrastinate. On the
other hand, tackle
procrastination in one area of
your life, and the other areas
will improve, too.

One of the biggest problems with
procrastination is that it is sneaky. For
example, the following are all good
things to do:

- Planning
- Prioritizing
- Learning

But they can also be a way to hide your
procrastination.

Do you spend a lot of time planning?
Some of that is probably
procrastination.

Do you reprioritize your to-do list
throughout the day? That is probably
procrastination.

If you repeatedly put off starting a project because you need to learn one more thing, that's procrastination.

Taking additional time to plan, prioritize or learn can be the right thing to do. Just be sure you aren't using it as a cover up for procrastination.

A simple way to reduce procrastination is to just be honest. When you are procrastinating, call it that instead of making excuses.

Bringing procrastination out in the open like this can be very effective in reducing its hold on you.

Action

You can have great ideas, a great plan and great intentions. But if you don't take action, none of it matters. Lack of action feeds your fears. To build confidence and get past your fears, take action.

Yes, action is important. But action without any planning means you might <u>not</u> be acting on the right things.

Years ago I worked with someone in the corporate world. When you first saw her working you were impressed. She had so much energy and appeared to be getting so much done.

But over time, a different picture appeared. There was a lot of activity, but not much accomplishment.

She worked on a lot of trivial things. She rarely completed a large task. Some of the large tasks were reassigned to someone else and others were just never completed.

Don't confuse activity with accomplishment.

Key Takeaways:

Planning is important, but don't spend so much time planning that it prevents you from taking action.

Action is key. Take it regularly.

Don't confuse activity with accomplishment.

Work on the right tasks and projects.

A simple way to reduce procrastination is to just be honest. When you are procrastinating, call it that instead of making excuses.

Here are five strategies to help you procrastinate less:

1. Think small and think now. Find the smallest step you can take and take it right now, this very minute.
2. Drop the perfectionism.
3. Move away from victim to empowered adult by changing the voice in your head:

   From:
   - I have to

- I better/should

To:
- I want to
- I prefer to

4. Take breaks often enough.
5. Limit distractions. For example, limit the number of programs and windows you have open on your computer at any given time.

Fearless *versus* Fear

Fearless

I hear many people talk about being fearless.

That's crap. There is no such thing. It's BS.

Fear is hard-wired into us. It's part of the fight-or-flight response that is stored in part of the brain known as the amygdala. This is one of the most primitive parts of our brain.

It's so primitive, that Seth Godin (and others) have called it the Lizard Brain.

Your goal isn't to become fearless. Your goal is to learn how to best manage your fear.

Fear

With fear, I encourage you to choose what I call the Third Option. We often get caught up in either-or thinking. That is, seeing only two options.

Instead, choose to look for the Third Option and you will usually find it. Sometimes you will find a fourth or fifth option too.

In this case, the obvious two choices are fight the fear or run from it. The Third Option is just to BE with the fear, to feel it fully.

Stay with the fear and be willing to feel the discomfort for a bit longer than you normally do. Do that you will get these benefits:

- You will be much more likely to make the change you want to make
- Each time you face fear in this way, you learn to manage it even better the next time
- All those ninnies talking about being fearless will be left in your trail of dust

Fear keeps you stuck. It prevents you from trying new things, from leaving your comfort zone.

> *"All great things start out as scary things, right?"*
> ~ from the movie Warm Bodies

Are you avoiding all scary things in your life? If so, you are putting limits on what you can achieve.

Let fear paralyze you and you won't take the action you want to take. If you fight the fear, the change likely won't happen either. So, what can you do?

In my late 20's I was working as a computer programmer and was extremely shy and quiet.

One morning I was enjoying a donut in the cafeteria with co-workers. We were approached by a guy from another department, Brent. He asked if any of us wanted to teach a class on computers through the local community college. I heard a voice say "sure." A moment later, I realized the voice was mine.

As soon as Brent left, my co-workers burst into laughter. I asked what was so funny and one of them said: "There is no way I can see you teaching a class. You can barely talk to us, how are you going to talk to a room of people you don't know?"

Everyone else at the table was nodding in agreement. They were right. I couldn't see how I would do it either.

But I knew I had to do it.

There were several reasons why. First, I believe in keeping my word. Second, I knew if I didn't do it, I would always wonder "what if." And third, I wanted to prove to my co-workers, and to myself, that I could do it.

The day arrived to teach and I found myself in front of a class of a dozen strangers.

I was a wreck.

My hands were trembling, my voice was quivering and my heart thumping. I was sweating.

Terrified and filled with fear, I wanted to run out of the room, but realized that would make things worse. After about ten minutes a strange thing happened.

I felt myself relax a little and noticed the fear started to fade, like a fog lifting. I sat down on the corner of the desk and the fear faded even more. After another five minutes I was telling jokes and laughing.

The fear was gone.

The class and I were completely engaged. Time seemed to stand still. I was in a state of flow[1].

Something that began as very difficult and stressful, turned into one of the best moments of my life. By staying with my discomfort longer than I wanted to I learned how to effectively deal with fear and move forward anyway.

Learning to stay with my fear is one of the most valuable skills I have ever learned. I have used it repeatedly over the last 30 years. I also discovered a love for teaching, something I enjoy to this day.

Whenever I have stuck with something I feared, I have always discovered something I love. Always.

---

[1] *Flow is a term coined by psychologist Mihaly Csikszentmihalyi. It has been defined as melding with an activity, where you experience spontaneous joy, bordering on rapture that is similar to an out of body experience.*

Fear is a compass showing you where to go. The things you resist out of fear, are important things. You resist <u>because</u> they are important. If they were not you would either just do them quickly or you would skip them completely.

I was filled with fear about teaching that class. But teaching was the exact thing I needed to do. My fear showed me what to pay attention to and act upon.

<u>Key Takeaways</u>:

Quit trying to be fearless. There is no such thing.

With fear, use The Third Option. Don't fight. Don't run. Just stay with the fear.

Fear is a compass showing you where to go.

Perfectionism *versus* Authenticity

Perfectionism

> *"The thing that is really hard, and really amazing, is giving up on being perfect and beginning the work of becoming yourself."*
> ~ Anna Quindlen

If you are a perfectionist you may not realize how much it costs you.

Perfectionism steals time. It limits your success by putting you in a box.

I am all for excellence. I am all for improving yourself. But that isn't perfectionism.

Perfectionism is unrealistic. Constantly chasing perfection robs you of precious time, and time is what life is made of. Whether we want to admit it or not, we all have a limited amount of time on this planet.

Yes, some things should be done with excellence. For example, whether you have your own business or work for someone else, customer service should always focus on excellence. In general, all relationships should be about excellence.

Not everything needs to be done with excellence, but some still need to be done well.

Other things don't even need to be done well, they can be done "good enough."

The key is to effectively decide which category to put each task in:

- Done with excellence
- Done well
- Done good enough

If you are a perfectionist, you spend extra time on each task. This limits the number of tasks you can take productive action on.

Finished is better than perfect.

Authenticity

What is your most valuable quality?

Your authenticity.

It isn't just important to let your authenticity shine through, it is crucial. The rest of us need you to be you.

Being the real you, helps you and it helps the rest of us, too.

You can only be your best self by being your real self.

Unfortunately, our school systems and workplaces are more about conformity than about being your own unique self.

It is drilled into us from a young age. Implanted into your mindset. Some people never question it their entire lives. They just keep on following the crowd.

I'm challenging you to question it.

Don't be different just to be different.
Simply be you. The real you.

Quit pretending to be someone you
aren't. We have all done it at some
point. I know I have. Eventually I
realized I just wanted to be me.

I call it moving from the "impress" stage
of life to the "express" stage of life.

That is, you become less concerned
about impressing others and more
concerned about expressing yourself.

When you aren't your true self it takes
up a lot of energy. Be your true self and
you will be surprised how much more
energy you have.

Part of being authentic is accepting your
failures and shortcomings.

If you think you have not failed much –
you are either fooling yourself or
playing it too safe. Those who rarely fail
are those who rarely try. There are only
three choices in life:

1. Failing often
2. Playing it too safe
3. Fooling yourself

Earlier in life I would have said I had not failed much. Now I see that was because I was using the last two choices almost exclusively. In time, I learned to use the first choice. The first choice is the best one – fail and fail often. Repeatedly avoiding failure, limits your chances to learn and grow.

It is easy to look at successful people and think they did not have failures along the way. Notice what J.K. Rowling, the author of the Harry Potter series, says about failure:

> *"Failure taught me things about myself that I could have learned no other way. I discovered that I had a strong will and more discipline than I had suspected; I also found out that I had friends whose value was truly above rubies."*

<u>Key Takeaways</u>:

Finished is better than perfect.

Authenticity is your most valuable quality.

You can only be your best self, by being your real self.

Repeatedly avoiding failure, limit your chances to learn and grow.

Fail and fail often, that's the path to success.

Don't be different just to be different. Simply be you. The real you.

Judgment *versus* Curiosity

Judgment

Years ago I heard a story about a man who was driving on a country road. A car approaching him was swerving all over the road.

As the car passed, he heard the driver yell "PIG." The man muttered to himself, "What a jerk! She has the nerve to call ME a pig when she's the one driving recklessly!"

As the man rounded a blind corner, his car crashed into a large pig.

Just like that man, we all judge others. It is easy to do without even realizing it. Think about when you are driving and someone cuts you off or tailgates you. It is easy to call them a jerk (or worse).

When we judge others it really says more about us than it says about them. When we judge others, we turn off:

- Patience
- Understanding
- Flexibility
- Curiosity
- Openness
- Learning

When we judge others we are acting from a place of self-importance and righteousness. The person you just judged, what do you really know about them?

The person tailgating you might have just received a call that one of their parents is on his or her deathbed. The person who cut you off in traffic, maybe they were distracted because they just found out they have cancer.

Judging others prevents you from learning. Suspend judgment. Stay curious. Learn something.

Curiosity

"It is a miracle that curiosity
survives formal education."
~ Albert Einstein

I was running errands and stopped for
lunch. As I sat down I noticed a family
near me with two young boys. The
youngest was so full of energy he would
not sit still. His behavior was scattered
and unfocused.

Suddenly he became focused. He went
to an empty table, grabbed a chair and
started to move it to his table. He was
about the same height as the chair,
making it very difficult for him to push
the chair across the carpet.

He did not complain or give up. He
simply put his head down and started
slowly pushing that chair across the
floor.

The scattered behavior was gone. He
was 100% focused, proceeding with

absolute certainty that he would succeed.

On a different day I may have ignored him by dismissing his behavior as annoying. Yet on that day I felt magnetized toward watching him. Why?

The main reason was I remained curious instead of judging his behavior or becoming negative.

When he grabbed the chair, I could have thought: Why doesn't he just go back to his own table? Instead I thought: I wonder what he is going to do?

The only way to continue to grow is through learning. The only way to learn is by staying open and curious.

Key Takeaways:

Research has shown that taking up a creative pursuit is one way to become less judgmental. What creative pursuit would you like to start?

Judging others prevents you from learning. Suspend judgment. Stay curious. Learn something.

Always Seeking Balance *versus* Living Your Purpose

Always Seeking Balance

Constantly trying to balance your life is overrated. It creates stress and is a huge waste of time.

Life, by its very nature, is unbalanced.

Having some sort of balance is good. But many have taken it too far, almost to the point of obsession.

There was a time when I thought what I wanted most was a balanced life. Those days are gone.

Think about the important moments in your life: graduation, falling in love, getting a job, getting married, having a child or completing a big project.

All of these events create unbalance. They require you to focus on them, while placing less emphasis on other things in your life.

Yes, you can have balance over the long-term. That's a good thing. But constantly trying to create balance in the short-term is counter-productive. Life is lived minute-to-minute.

Picture a baby girl taking her first steps. She leans forward, in an unbalanced way. She falls and prevents the fall by jabbing one foot forward to catch herself. Then she falls again and catches herself with the other foot. Walking is a series of unbalanced movements.

Focusing too much on balancing your life creates unnecessary stress. The preoccupation with balance can also cause you to overlook opportunities that are right in front of you.

Don't get so preoccupied with always trying to create balance that you miss out on the special moments in life.

Living Your Purpose

Live your purpose. Love your purpose. If you aren't, you have lost your purpose.

If you aren't living your purpose, you are swimming upstream. Your life will be more complicated and more difficult.

Overall, it will be harder for you to succeed and be fulfilled.

We all have a purpose. Do you know yours?

People often get their expectations a bit sideways when it comes to finding their calling or purpose in life. Derek Sivers says it well in his fabulous book *Anything You Want*:

> *"If you think your life's purpose needs to hit you like a lightning bolt you'll overlook the little day-to-day things that fascinate you."*

Don't expect your purpose to be revealed to you in some grand way. It probably won't be.

More likely it will come to you in the quiet moments. It may appear in very subtle ways and only be revealed a little at a time. This doesn't make your purpose any less important. It is very important.

Your purpose doesn't have to come to you in a special way for it to be special.

We all crave meaning in our lives. Knowing and living your purpose is how to find that meaning.

Inject your life with purpose and everything else falls into place: relationships, love, happiness, joy and peace. If you are disconnected from your purpose, there will always be an uneasiness. You will feel like something is missing because something *is* missing.

"If you lose your purpose, it's like you're broken."
~ from the movie Hugo

Most of us knew our purpose at one time or another. Often it gets drilled out of us by family, school or society. When we are children, others often discourage us from following our purpose. Maybe you heard things like:

- Be more practical.
- You can't make money doing THAT!
- Get your head out of the clouds.

Regardless of what you were told or what you came to believe, you do have a purpose. There is something you were meant to do. It is critical to your success and fulfillment that you find it and do it. Don't be selfish; share it with the rest of us.

Steven Pressfield says it well:

"We're not born with unlimited choices. We can't be anything we want to be. We come into this world with a specific, personal destiny. We have a job to do, a calling to enact, a self to become."

Connect with your purpose and make your life more meaningful.

Key Takeaways:

Constantly trying to balance your life is overrated. It creates stress and is a huge waste of time.

Life, by its very nature, is unbalanced.

Live your purpose. Love your purpose. If you aren't, you have lost your purpose.

Don't expect your purpose to be revealed to you in some grand way. Your purpose doesn't have to come to you in a special way for it to be special.

Weaknesses *versus* Strengths

<u>Weaknesses</u>

By weaknesses, I mean things that drain your energy, making you feel weaker. They aren't necessarily the things you are bad at.

From the time you enter school and in most workplaces, you are conditioned to work on your weaknesses.

It becomes part of your mindset to constantly be working on your weaknesses.

That's a bad idea.

Your weaknesses drain your energy. Why would you want to spend a significant amount of time draining your energy?

There is nothing wrong with working to improve yourself, but I am talking about the bigger picture here. Do not spend significant time trying to get really good at something that does not appeal to you or that drains your energy.

Time spent on your weaknesses will provide little payback. That is, you will only improve a little.

But time spent on your strengths, that's a different story…

Strengths

> "…keep sharpening your strengths
> and make them so powerful that they
> render your weaknesses irrelevant"
> ~ Marcus Buckingham

By strengths, I mean the things that energize you, making you feel stronger. They aren't necessarily the things you are good at.

For example, for many years I worked in Information Technology and I was good at it.

In time, I realized I didn't get an energy boost from that work specifically. I got energized from learning new things, helping others and solving problems.

Did I get to do those things as part of my IT job? Early in my career, I did. Over time, those things happened less frequently. As a result, I became less interested in my work.

As a trainer, speaker and coach, I use all three of these strengths regularly. My professional life is much more satisfying because I get to use my strengths often.

Your strengths are your competitive advantage. Leverage your time by spending the majority of time where you are strong. You will succeed much more rapidly.

Team up with people who are good at what you are weak at. The best teams are ones where everyone is playing to his or her own strengths.

Key Takeaways:

Spending significant time on your weaknesses is a waste of time.

Spend as much time as possible with your strengths. They are your competitive advantage.

Multitasking *versus* Single Focus

Multitasking

Multitasking is a way to screw up multiple tasks at the same time.

It might just take the award for the mindset that is farthest off base.

All scientific research on multitasking concludes the same thing: it is highly inefficient. Not some of the research, all of it!

Before you get upset or call me a quack, let's define what multitasking is, and isn't.

Let's say you are working on your computer and print a long document. While the document is printing, you read some email. That isn't multitasking, because you aren't focusing on both tasks at the same time. You have quit doing one task while you go to do the other. This is efficient use of your time.

Multitasking is when you try to:

- Do two or more tasks at the same time that both require mental focus, or
- Rapidly switch between tasks that both require mental focus

For example, multitasking is when you continue to read emails during a phone conversation. You are giving partial attention to both tasks, doing each more poorly than if you did them separately.

If you still do not believe that multitasking is a big waste of time, do the following exercise from Dave Crenshaw.

He wrote a wonderful book: *The Myth of Multitasking*.

Go to this link and print the 1-page pdf:

davecrenshaw.com/multitasking-exercise.pdf

This pdf contains the exercise and instructions.

It's a two-part exercise. You will need to time each part. The idea is to do each as quickly as you can.

It won't take long. Do it right now.

Are you surprised by your times? Most people are.

For most, the multitasking part takes roughly twice as long as the other section.

This is a very simple task, clearly defined and you know exactly what is coming next. Even so, your efficiency took a big hit.

Imagine how much more your efficiency drops with something as complex and unpredictable as a phone conversation combined with any other task.

Stop fooling yourself. Multitasking is a waste of time. The sooner you limit it in your life, the more productive you will be.

Single Focus

The brain is often compared to a computer. That isn't an accurate comparison.

A computer multitasks by rapidly switching from one task to another, giving the *appearance* that multiple things are happening at once. They really aren't.

A computer can do this rapid switching with little loss of efficiency and without losing track of where it was with each task.

Your brain cannot.

When you try to multitask, you are fooling yourself, thinking you are doing two things at once.

In reality your brain is rapidly switching back and forth. It happens so quickly you aren't even aware of it.

When you do this, your brain will be significantly less efficient. You may also lose track of where you are with either, or both, tasks. If so, efficiency takes an even bigger hit.

Your brain can only focus on one thought at a time. Research has proven this repeatedly. One thought a time, that's it.

But what about walking while you talk on the phone? Isn't that two things at once?

It isn't because the walking is happening in the background: you aren't consciously focusing on it.

If you still doubt me, think of a time you were walking and talking on the phone and someone asked you a complicated question or said something surprising.

You automatically stopped walking, didn't you? This happened without even consciously thinking, "stop walking."

Your brain knew the conversation required your full attention, so it automatically shut down anything else it could (in this case, walking).

When you juggle multiple mental tasks your brain often loses track of where you were. Even if it doesn't lose track, your brain still requires time to get back to the same level of concentration.

When you ask your brain to constantly switch between multiple tasks, you are repeatedly draining your efficiency.

Sophie Leroy has discovered another reason why multitasking is a drain.

She is a business professor at the University of Minnesota. Through her research, she has coined the term "attention residue."

Her research has uncovered that when you switch from one task to another, your attention doesn't immediately follow. That is, a residue of your attention remains stuck thinking about the original task.

So when you repeatedly switch back and forth during multitasking, attention residue means there is an even more significant drain on your efficiency.

The more time you dedicate toward a single-focus, the more productive you will be.

<u>Key Takeaways</u>:

Multitasking is a way to screw up multiple tasks at the same time.

The sooner you limit multitasking in your life, the more productive you will be.

Single task your work to be more productive and produce higher quality work.

Approval from Others *versus* Self-Acceptance

Approval from Others

Think back to your childhood. If you were like most children, you tried to gain approval from your parents in order to earn their love. This can continue into adulthood: tying your sense of self-worth to approval from others: spouse, other family members, friends, etc.

Looking externally for your sense of self-worth is a losing game.

The only way to consistently feel positive self-worth is to find it internally.

Self-Acceptance

> *"We've each learned to be delighted with what we are."*
> ~ James T. Kirk

Are you delighted with what you are?

We all have our moments where we feel pretty darn good about ourselves. But being delighted about it maybe does not happen often.

We each tend to be our own worst critic. We see our own shortcomings in a much harsher light than most everyone around us.

If we were as critical of our friends as we are of ourselves, we probably would not have any friends.

Be more accepting of yourself and you become a better version of yourself.

Choose to be gentler with yourself. Become your own best friend.

<u>Key Takeaways</u>:

Looking externally for your sense of self-worth is a losing game.

The only way to consistently feel positive self-worth is to find it internally.

Be more accepting of yourself and you become a better version of yourself.

Chasing Happiness *versus* Doing What You Love

Chasing Happiness

If you are chasing happiness, your mindset needs an adjustment. Happiness is rarely achieved directly.

I recently searched the book section of amazon.com for "happiness." It returned more than 93,000 matches.

Chasing happiness has almost become a sickness. People are stressed out about happiness, thinking they need to find it or find more of it.

Ironically, if they quit trying so hard to find happiness, they might actually be happier.

Some people see happiness as a starting point. Their mindset is: think happy thoughts, act in a happy manner and you will be happy.

Others have a mindset that sees happiness as an ending point, a goal to reach. Happiness becomes a destination.

Both approaches miss the mark. Happiness is in the middle.

If you have been chasing happiness, here is the mindset shift I recommend. It is a simple three-step approach:

1. Start by doing what you love to do.
2. By doing what you love, happiness will be a natural by-product.
3. From that happiness will spring success. That success will create more happiness.

In other words, do not seek out happiness. Instead, find what you love to do and focus on it. Spend time doing what you love and happiness will find you. Others will see how engaged and happy you are and this will help draw the right people into your life, helping you to be more successful.

Doing What You Love

When you do what you love, happiness is a natural by-product. People will notice your joy and dedication and want to be a part of it.

A big part of what makes you, YOU, is what you love to do. Maybe you have been hiding it. It is safer to hide what you love to do. There is less chance to be criticized about it. It keeps what you love to do safe; and if you have hidden it for years then it is even easier to keep hiding it.

Fear can prevent you from doing what you love. The best approach with fear is to take small steps. Express what you love to do in small ways at first until it feels more comfortable.

You may be thinking this sounds great, but:

a) There is no way I can make money doing what I love, or
b) I can't figure out what I love to do

First, stop thinking you <u>have</u> to make money doing what you love to do. You don't. This mindset is limiting and it is holding you back.

Instead, make time to do what you love. Once you start doing what you love, you may discover an entirely new way to make money with it. Even if you don't, you are still doing what you love, and that is a beautiful thing.

Second, if you are unsure what you love to do, try this exercise. Ask close friends or family members to help you. Tell them you are trying to find out what you truly love. For several weeks, have them pay extra close attention to your eyes and body language when you are speaking.

At some point they will see a shift in you – a change in posture and a certain look in your eyes. You will "light up." They may even notice you talking so fast you barely get the words out quickly enough.

Whatever you are talking about, this is what you love.

But here is the catch: it may <u>not</u> be the exact thing you are talking about.

For example, let's say you "light up" when you are talking about cooking. It may be cooking itself that you love or it may be what cooking represents to you: social gatherings, happy times, etc.

Write down whatever it is that lights you up and also write down what you enjoy about it.

Study these lists and you will begin to see patterns. Within those patterns you will find the thing(s) you love to do.

Key Takeaways:

Happiness is in the middle.

You don't have to make money doing what you love.

Spend time doing what you love and happiness will find you.

The Easy Life *versus* A Life With Challenges

The Easy Life

It is only natural to want life to be easy. But with the easy life you stop learning and growing.

An easy life loses meaning and purpose.

Think of the people you admire the most. Think of the people you know who have made the biggest impact on you and others.

Have these people always had an easy life? I doubt it.

When I think about the people I admire the most, all of them have overcome a difficult challenge.

They have come out the other side of that challenge, stronger, more resilient and smarter. They are better prepared for the next challenge.

An easy life teaches you nothing. Challenges are your classroom.

A Life With Challenges

For me, 2011 was a year of ups and downs: relocating across country and changing careers by launching my business full-time.

The year had plenty of challenges and blessings. In time, I discovered that both were blessings.

But while I was in the middle of a challenge, nothing about it felt like a blessing.

When faced with a challenge, my initial thought was I'm stuck without any options. But I discovered some wonderful surprises:

- My inner resourcefulness is much stronger than I realized.
- The challenge was simply a chance to be more creative.

- There were people who were willing and able to help, but in my first attempt I had not thought of asking them. Simply asking for their help opened up many new possibilities.

My options were only limited by my own limited thinking.

Also, with each challenge, my thinking became increasingly more open. Each challenge became easier to confront than the previous one, because I learned to shift my mindset to see that challenges have a positive aspect to them.

Let me share a wonderful story about a carrot, an egg and a coffee bean (author unknown):

Put a carrot, an egg and a coffee bean in hot water and each reacts differently. Think of the hot water as symbolizing the challenges in your life. When a challenge enters your life which are you? A carrot: getting soft when tough things happen; an egg, hardening yourself to life's challenges; or a coffee bean, using the challenge to transform yourself into something new and better?

When I started college, I didn't know what to major in. I was always good at math and science and my older brother was an engineer, so I gave that a try.

Toward the end of my freshman year I received an "F" on an exam. My grades had always been good, so at that moment I saw myself as a complete failure. As I walked across campus, I felt like my life had lost all meaning.

The "F" helped me see I had not taken the time to decide on a field of study. I was just doing what was easiest. Even though I took the class over and earned an "A," the "F" prompted me to search for another major. My search uncovered both technology and teaching. I had a long, rewarding career in the field of technology. Teaching is something I love and continue to do even now.

Instead of my life losing meaning, the challenge of the "F" helped me find meaning.

You need challenges. Avoiding challenges keeps you stuck. The path to a better life is <u>through</u> challenges, not by avoiding them.

Shift your mindset and transform challenges into one of your biggest allies. Challenges can light the way for improvement, learning and growth.

Les Parrott tells a great story in his book, *3 Seconds - The Power of Thinking Twice*:

> *"A mother Angolan Giraffe will kick a newborn off its feet. If the newborn stops trying to get up, the mother kicks it until it does get up. Once it gets up again, the mother kicks it off its feet again."*

Why would the mother giraffe do this?

She is training the newborn to get up in the wild. If the newborn doesn't learn this critical skill at any early age, it will be easy prey.

How often do we feel like this newborn giraffe, wondering why we keep getting kicked?

Maybe the kicks are preparing us for what lies ahead.

Challenges force you to focus. They help you learn and adapt.

It is no coincidence that overcoming challenges is a common thread among successful people.

Challenges stretch you, giving you a chance to be more resourceful and learn new things. Challenges force you to find a new path. Many times it is an improvement over the original path.

Use small challenges as a training ground for dealing with larger ones.

You always have a choice with challenges. Use them as a way to better yourself.

<u>Key Takeaways</u>:

An easy life teaches you nothing. Challenges are your classroom.

Your options are limited more by your limited thinking than by the challenges you face.

Avoiding challenges keeps you stuck.

Challenges force you to focus. They help you learn and adapt.

If you are still skeptical that challenges can help you, do the following exercise. The next time a challenge shows up, write about it. It doesn't have to be lengthy. A short note or a few bullet points will work.

Make a note on your calendar for one month from that day to read what you wrote.

As you read it a month later, write down anything positive that came from it.

Do this again a few months later. I think you will be amazed at what you find. I know I was.

Wishing Life Was Different *versus* Gratitude for What Is

Wishing Life Was Different

We all want our lives to be good. I get it.

But wishing for your life to be different is a never-ending game. Life will never be perfect. There will always be something you don't like.

Think back to the last chapter and the story of the giraffe. I imagine that baby giraffe was wishing its life was different, that the mother wasn't kicking it. If it got its wish, what's the result? It would be lunch for some predator.

Be careful what you wish for. The so-called negative things in our lives help us a lot more than we realize.

Accepting your life as it is – good and bad – takes maturity and wisdom. It helps you move forward.

Gratitude for What Is

It is easy to be grateful for good things. How many of us are grateful when things don't go well?

It's not easy, but the idea is to be in a constant state of gratitude, regardless of the situation.

> *"Our pain can be our greatest teacher. It leads us to places we'd never go on our own."*
> ~ Debbie Ford

When I was young, my father died suddenly. I have felt the pain of divorce. I know the sorrow of being estranged from my daughter. Do I wish these events had played out differently? Absolutely.

But in each of these cases I learned valuable lessons. I am grateful for the lessons.

From my dad's passing, I learned to:

- Never take loved ones for granted
- Be grateful my mom is still living; some people have lost both parents
- Be grateful my dad lived as long as he did - some have never known their father at all

Through divorce, I learned:

- Better decisions are made when you use both your head and your heart
- How to love and respect myself, so I can better love and respect another person
- A relationship can't thrive based upon just love (you need to like, respect and understand each other, too)

Being deprived of a relationship with my daughter - words can't accurately express the depth of that pain.

In time I saw this experience taught me:

- True love is expressing your feelings, regardless of whether the other person will express their feelings
- Focus less on the outcome and more on making sure I have done the best I am able to
- When I have given my best effort, it is time to have faith and trust that things will work out

I wish these events had played out differently. Yet, I am grateful for what I have learned and for the significant personal and spiritual growth I have experienced as a result.

The growth only happened because I chose to shift my mindset.

I could have adopted a mindset of "poor me." What would that have looked like? I would have moped around feeling sorry for myself or shut myself off emotionally, pretending these things didn't happen.

Those might be helpful ways to cope in the short-term, but not in the long-term.

Eventually, I chose a mindset where I actively looked for what I could learn from each challenge.

<u>Key Takeaways</u>:

Accepting your life as it is – good and bad – takes maturity and wisdom.

Choose a mindset that allows you to be grateful no matter the outcome. Learn to be in a constant state of gratitude

Control *versus* Letting Go

Control

We all like to feel in control. It is easy to blur the lines between what we can control and what we can't. Most things are outside of our control.

Some years ago I was fed up with being indecisive about making a career change.

I was done talking about it, ready to take action. I decided to leave my Information Technology job and start my own business.

I enrolled in an online university to get my Master's degree in psychology.

Shortly after I enrolled, major changes took place at my workplace: reorganizations, layoffs, higher hour expectations and a big spike in stress levels.

To find time for school and the extra work hours, I quit exercising, spent less time with friends, slept fewer hours and ate more junk food/fast food.

The more I tried to control everything, the worse it got. I gained a bunch of weight, was sleep-deprived and overly stressed.

I was heading down a very dark path. Something had to give.

I decided to let go, to quit school. At first it felt like a failure, like I had given up on the career change.

Almost immediately it was clear it was a great decision. My life improved in many ways. I was much less stressed, eating better and sleeping better. It felt great to exercise again and enjoy time with friends. I lost the weight, was healthier and happier.

Letting go was clearly the best decision.

The career change still happened and it was only a little different than my original plan.

Letting Go

I love to inline skate. A few years back on a gorgeous fall day I decided to go for a skate. After 20 minutes I saw many dark clouds moving in. I turned around and headed back toward home. [2]

The wind picked up. I skated faster. It looked like I might get home before the rain. Then I heard thunder. I continued with the quick pace.

A few blocks from home, I got caught in a downpour. I stopped, pulled off my skates and socks and walked the rest of the way.

The temperature had dropped a lot. The rain was cold. I was drenched to the

---

[2] *Inline skating just doesn't work with wet pavement. You will either "do the splits" or pull a muscle.*

point that my glasses fogged over. I had to take them off to see anything.

At this point, I was laughing very hard, imagining what a sight I must have been.

As I zig-zagged barefoot through the rain, squinting, carrying skates, socks, and glasses I felt completely alive! I was fully present in that moment. I was joyously celebrating the madness and loving it.

Instead of reacting with anger, frustration or disappointment, I let go and surrendered to the rain. Because I surrendered, the rainstorm became a blessing to me.

Key Takeaways:

Letting go is sometimes the best way to get what you want.

If a situation gets worse the more you try to control it, then maybe it is time to let go.

Have a mindset that recognizes letting go as a viable option.

Certainty *versus* Adaptability

Certainty

Very few things in life are certain. Yet we often fool ourselves into thinking they are.

A few years ago, as I was leaving the library, a woman with two small children was ahead of me. It started to rain. It was not raining hard, but the large drops gave the feeling that a downpour might cut loose at any time. Even though she had a very close parking spot, the woman was agitated, urging the kids to hurry so they didn't get wet. The kids became agitated.

As I continued to walk to my car, I noticed another woman putting a stroller away in her van. She was singing some little verse about the rain and grinning from ear to ear.

Each woman dealt with uncertainty differently. The first woman was rushed and agitated. The second, smiling and joyous, was ready to embrace uncertainty. Which mindset would you rather have?

Adaptability

> *"Water is fluid, soft, and yielding. But water will wear away rock, which is rigid and cannot yield. As a rule, whatever is fluid, soft, and yielding will overcome whatever is rigid and hard. This is another paradox: what is soft is strong."* ~ Lao Tzu

This is ancient wisdom from Lao Tzu (600 BC). Have you stopped to see how you are approaching your life, rigid versus flexible?

Being rigid isn't all bad. It is good to have certain values and principles in your life that are fixed. But be rigid in too many areas and it will hold you back.

Staying fluid, like water, opens up new possibilities. Look at where your life is rigid and decide if more flexibility might help.

For example, when setting goals, it is easy to get into a fixed mindset. Why not be more fluid with your goals, more adaptable?

Whatever your goals are, re-evaluate them every month or two. You might want to ask these types of questions:

- Has a new goal surfaced that should replace one (or more) of my other goals?
- Did I break my goals down into small enough steps?
- Are there any goals I should delete?

People are often hesitant to delete goals. I say if it is no longer serving you, then delete it. Re-vamping your goals can be very energizing. Life isn't static don't let your goals be static.

Key Takeaways:

Create a mindset that is open to uncertainty.

Be fluid and adaptable, like water.

Life isn't static don't let your goals be static.

Stuck in Your Comfort Zone *versus* Active Learning

Stuck in Your Comfort Zone

Comfort Zones have gotten a bad rap.

There is much talk about how important it is to get out of your comfort zone.

I agree with that…to a point.

You can become stuck in your comfort zone, staying there simply because it's easy. That can be a bad thing.

But your comfort zone isn't a bad place.

Earlier I talked about leveraging your strengths instead of spending a ton of time trying to improve your weaknesses.

Where do you think your strengths are? In your comfort zone.

If you are in your comfort zone to use your strengths, stay right there. It's a great place for you to be.

But, if you are there to avoid change and resist learning anything new, it's time to step out.

Active Learning

When is the best time to upgrade your skills, learn something new or better yourself in some way?

Now is always a good time to do those things.

Many people have recently upgraded their skills. If you aren't one of them, you are being left in the dust.

What do you want or need to learn? What have you put in place to begin that learning? What are you waiting for?

I graduated some years back from the University of Northern Iowa (UNI). While there, UNI implemented a writing competency exam. To graduate, you had to pass the test. As I finished the test, I thought I had done okay. I bombed it.

The good news: I could take it again. The bad news: Time was running out; it was nearly the end of my junior year.

I didn't want to fail again. I found everything I could on how to be a better writer. I started studying immediately.

My efforts paid off. I passed the test on the next try.

My studying produced an interesting side benefit. Even though I'd passed the test, I still wanted to learn more about writing. As I learned more, I developed a real love of writing.

This one decision, choosing to improve my writing, created many significant, positive benefits for me.

For example, I managed people in the corporate world for 20 years. My improved writing skills helped me be a more effective manager.

I developed and taught an adult education class on writing. Teaching this class allowed me to meet new people and improve my public speaking skills.

I started my own blog. At one point I was writing two blogs. My love for writing has not faded.

By doing more than just the minimum, I found an activity I love that has helped me both professionally and personally.

Key Takeaways:

Now is always a good time to upgrade your skills or learn something new.

If you are in your comfort zone to use your strengths, stay right there.

If you are in your comfort zone to avoid change, it's time to step out.

Focusing on the Past or the Future *versus* Focusing on the Present

Focusing on the Past or the Future

If your mindset is too focused on the past or future, you will have problems. Don't be absent from the present.

There may be decisions from your past you wish you had handled differently. Maybe there are difficult events from your past you wish hadn't happened at all.

Either way, regretting the past keeps you stuck in the past, missing out on the present.

The past is great for fond memories and for learning from mistakes. Other than that, it holds little value.

The future is great for planning and anticipating future events. Other than that, it holds little value.

Worry or anxiety about the future does not change the future. It only makes the present less pleasant.

Focusing on the Present

The present holds a lot of value.

Real action only happens in the present.

People often forget this.

People often talk about future action like they are really doing something. It may be a great plan, but at this point it is just talk and nothing more.

Sometimes I hear people talk about the past like they are going to change it.

The reality is:

- Past action = just a memory
- Future action = just a plan
- Present action = real action

To be successful and productive, focus on the present.

The present is the only place where you can take action.

<u>Key Takeaways</u>:

Regretting the past keeps you stuck in the past, missing out on the present.

Worry or anxiety about the future does not change the future. It only makes the present less pleasant.

Don't be absent from the present.

To be successful and productive focus on the present.

Real action only happens in the present.

Acknowledgements

I want to thank my sister, Linda Augustine, for the help and support you have given me over the years in both my personal and professional journeys. You have truly made a difference.

Also, thanks to Robbi Hess for her editing skills and to Susan Veach for designing such a beautiful cover.

There are many other friends and family that have helped me at various stages of my life -- too many to mention here. Your support through the tough times and laughter during the good times is worth more than I can ever express.

And lastly I want to thank my parents, Harry and Dorothy Wilson. Even though you both came from humble and difficult beginnings, you always gave your best. I thank you for bringing me into this world and for all you taught me. In particular, thank you for teaching me: persistence, loyalty and the power of laughter to connect and heal.

Printed by CreateSpace, an Amazon.com Company

Other Books by Bob Wilson

Divorce:
>   Learning to Heal and Grow

Toss Those Resolutions:
>   Why It's Time to Give Them Up
>   and What to Do Instead

Woody Two Shoes:
>   New Shoes For Woody

About the Author

Bob Wilson learned a lot by flunking a writing competency exam in college. He learned how to improve his writing skills. He also learned that he loves to write.

For over 20 years Bob has enjoyed helping people grow and achieve more. He has a passion for inspiring others to succeed.

He is the author of multiple books and has a background in education, management, coaching and technology.

Bob loves to travel, meet new people, experience new things and listen to live music. He lives in sunny Phoenix, Arizona.

You can contact Bob via email at: bobwilson7711@gmail.com

Made in the USA
San Bernardino, CA
08 November 2017